# Prayers for Women Who Can't Pray

# Prayers for Women Who Can't Pray

by

Katharine Smithrim
and Melanie Craig-Hansford

*For Gretta — with our heartfelt thanks for your beautiful and generous words on the back cover!*

WINTERGREEN
STUDIOS PRESS

*Katharine*     *Melanie*

**Wintergreen Studios Press**
P.O. Box 75, Yarker, ON, Canada K0K 3N0

Book design by Rena Upitis
Illustrations and cover painting by Claire Grady-Smith
Front cover design by Rena Upitis
Composed in Book Antiqua and Candara, typefaces designed by Monotype Typography and Gary Munch, respectively

**Library and Archives Canada Cataloguing in Publication**
Smithrim, Katharine Louise, 1950 —
Craig-Hansford, Melanie, 1962 —

Prayers for Women Who Can't Pray/Katharine Smithrim and Melanie Craig-Hansford

ISBN-10: 0986547360 EAN-13: 978-0986547362

1. Body, Mind, Spirit — General.

I.   Title. Prayers for Women Who Can't Pray

Legal Deposit – Library and Archives Canada

# Table of Contents

# Introduction

This is a book of prayers for women who want to pray but can't. Many women feel the urge to pray — when a child is sick, when a loved one is dying, when relationships sour, in the presence of beauty. Our impulse is to say "Oh God, help!" or "Oh God, thank you." But as soon as we think or say the word *God*, many of us freeze, because we do not believe in a god who intervenes in our lives.

We may well believe that there is a spiritual dimension or that life is imbued with the sacred. We may believe in a timeless, mysterious grace that envelops us all. Yet the very word *God* and the concept of prayer may have lost meaning for us. However, even when our image of divinity is not of a god who helps us, who wants to be thanked and praised, or who judges or forgives us, it is still possible to pray and to think about what prayer means.

Prayer becomes a response to the mystery of life. The urge to pray comes from our overwhelming need to express gratitude, our longing for serenity, our concern for loved ones, and our need for light in dark places.

And so we pray.

A simple shift in language represents a profound shift in how we conceive of prayer. Instead of saying "Thank you, God, for this beautiful day," we can say "May I be filled with gratitude for this beautiful day." The *May I* is not asking permission, as in, "May I have one of these books?" Rather we use it in the sense of "May it be so." It places the responsibility on ourselves to pay attention to the day, be grateful for that day, and honour it with the way we live it.

Instead of saying "Oh God, keep my child safe," we might say "May grace protect my child, this hour, this day, and all through the night." We are calling on the spiritual world, some holy mystery, a timeless grace, a divine spark within, to attend our child. All those images of the divine have been meaningful to people at various times in history and have been named *God*. Some women can still use the word *God*. Many cannot.

In this book, we offer the kinds of prayers we can still pray. There are one-line prayers, easy to memorize, and to think or say at all times of the day and night, such as when we go to bed, enter our workplace, or wait for the hand dryer to dry our hands. We can write them on cards and put them up on walls, cupboards, and mirrors to be there when we need them. There are also longer prayers to read when we have the time to be still. There are prayers to be read in community, and finally, there is a prayer ritual, like a rosary, to be used with prayer stones you can keep with you in your pocket or bag.

We hope that you can pray these prayers, that this prayerful language is meaningful for you, and that you might begin to shape your days with your own authentic and sustaining words of prayer.

Katharine Smithrim
Melanie Craig-Hansford
Kingston, Ontario
February 2012

# Short Prayers

## Morning Prayer

I greet this day. May love light my way, and may life's energy sustain me the whole day through.

## Sunny Morning

Blessed be the morning. May the sun's glow warm the earth beneath my feet. May its energy surround me as I face this new day.

## Rainy Morning

Blessed be the morning. As the rain nourishes the earth, may it nourish my soul.

## Evening Prayer

As this day comes to an end, may the lengthening shadows cast peace and quiet over my spirit, that I may embrace the night.

## Going to Sleep

Now I lay me down to sleep. I give over the thoughts and worries of this day to the healing grace of this night.

## Leaving Home for the Day

As I leave my home, may I pause to feel the freshness and energy that greet me.

## Arriving at Work

As I open the door to my workplace, I breathe in life's energy. May it carry me through this day.

## Competence

May I enjoy my capacity to move through my tasks lightly and deftly.

## Working with Others

May my demeanor and the quality of my interactions reassure my colleagues of my good will and respect.

## Returning Home from Work

As I return home, may I leave work behind and greet my family open to renewal and affection.

## Night Blessing for a Child

Blessings on this beloved child. May sweet sleep attend him/her all through the night.

## Saying Good-bye to a Loved One

Good-bye, my beloved. May life's energy sustain you, grace protect you, and love light your way until we are together again.

## Gratitude for Beauty

My cup is full. I am filled with gratitude for the beauty of _____.

## Waiting for Hands to Dry at a Hand-Dryer

I am grateful to you, my hands, for your healing and holding and helping.

## Going Back to Sleep

It is the middle of the night. I want to go back to sleep. May peace creep into my body as I breathe in acceptance and breathe out frustration.

## When I Am Ill

I am tired and sick. May I gather strength one minute at a time, as I breathe in courage and breathe out fear.

## When Someone is Ill

_____is tired and sick. May she/he feel the healing energy of life that envelops us all.

## When Life Is Hard

Life is hard today. May the healing energy of the sun be present in my mind, body, and spirit this minute, this hour, this day, and all through the coming night.

Life is hard for _____. May the healing energy of the sun be present in his/her mind, body and spirit this minute, this hour, this day, and all through the coming night.

## Aging

May I listen to my body: its longings, its aches, its stiffness, its pains.
May I be still and trust that the wisdom I need to guide me forward will come.

## Paying Attention

I stop now to think about what I am doing. May I stay present and resist the urge to do more than one thing at a time. May I know the deep joy that comes from paying loving attention.

## Water

I give thanks for water—water that sustains my life and all life on this planet.

## Air

Spirit of life and living, divine breath, breathe me whole and breathe me joy.

## Fire

Oh fire! Warm my face, warm my body, warm my heart, that I, in turn, may warm the world.

## Wind

Wind. Blow through my spirit and leave me gaping

## My Blessings

May I be ever mindful of my blessings. May I see how they shape my experience and be grateful.

## How I Live

May I be ever mindful that how I live touches unknown shores.

## Garden

Blessed be my garden. May the grace it bestows on me find a home in my spirit.

## Gardening

May I honour the joy of dirty fingernails, calluses, and stiff muscles as I work to create beauty and nourishment.

## Children of the World

I pray for the world's children, for those far away and those close to home. May I live my life in a way that honours children.

## Injustice

As I encounter injustice near and far, may I discover what calls me to respond with commitment and passion.

## War

I pray that daily habits of understanding and generosity in ordinary people will overcome war and religious strife.

## Namaste

May I honour that which is sacred within you.

## Wine

With gratitude I drink this wine. May I remember the soil, the light, the warmth, the rain, and the work that have brought this wine to my table.

## Blessing on a Meal

Blessed be the sun, the rain, and the hands that have brought this food to my/our table.

## Before Reading a Book

May I open my mind as I open this book. May the words bring me insight.

## Paying Bills

In gratitude, I remind myself that it is through my hard work and perseverance that I can pay this bill.

## No Money to Pay Bills

I am in trouble. I need help. May I seek and find wise counsel.

## Anger

May I remain grateful for the insight that my anger provides. May I have the strength to confront the injustices that rage in our world.

## Loneliness

I feel alone and sad. May the energy that sustains life lift me up and wrap me round.

## Fatigue

I am so tired. Fatigue has taken my energy and my humour. May I breathe in strength to carry me forward until I can rest.

## Rest

Now that I can rest, may I enjoy this rest in every cell of my body and be grateful for the gift of renewal.

## Joy

I invite into my life the things that bring me joy. I acknowledge and name them. May this honouring in turn bring joy to the people around me.

## Forgiveness

May I come to know the healing power of forgiveness, remembering that when I forgive myself, it frees me to forgive others.

# Longer Prayers

## A Holy Thread

A holy thread weaves itself through all of us.
I give thanks for that sacred fibre.

The same holy thread weaves itself through
everything around us:
> the bark on the trees
> the grains of sand on the beach
> the strands of a spider web
> the sunset.

I give thanks for the sacred fiber that unites
human and non-human,
animate and inanimate,
solid and spirit.

## Different Gods

The timeless grace that surrounds us has been personified, given human gender and many names: God, Goddess, Allah, Sophia, Yahweh.
Blessed are those names and faces.

May I be ever open to the wisdom that other points of view grant me.

May I be ever open to the beauty in the imagery that other theologies have given humankind.

May I keep my mind and heart open to the insight that other perspectives present to the world.

Blessed are our differences.

## A Fireside Prayer

Nourishing flame
I bring an offering of troubles
and place it on the hearth.

May the ascending flame carry away my worries
Wrap me in comforting warmth
Replenish me
And lead me to quiet evenings and silent stars.

## Springtime Walk in the Woods

Blessed be my silent stroll
through this spring forest.

Blessed be the new growth
peeking through the ground cover.

Blessed be the white trilliums
washing the woods with joy.

Blessed be the multitude of birds
singing away the wintery silence.

Blessed be the tree buds
trembling with new energy.

Blessed be new beginnings.

## A Blessing for Winter

In the cold, dark days of winter,
When I long for light and sunshine on my face,
Let me find brightness in other places:

> The glow of a fire
> The brilliance in my friend's eyes when we laugh
> The clarity of the ice on the lake
> The million sparkles of sun on the snow.

## Solid Ground

May I find comfort in the solid things that keep me grounded.

> The stone I hold in my hand
> The earth beneath my feet
> The wooden rocker on my porch
> The climbing tree in my yard
> The laughter of my children
> The smile on my lover's face.

## Creativity

I call forth the creative energies within me.

I call forth the creative energies that flow through me.

I call forth the collective imagination that inspires
new perspectives, new insights, new interpretations
and new innovations.

May I have the courage to let go of fear and doubt.

Blessed be my inner vision.

## A Declaration of My Individuality

Let me proclaim out loud
that I will sing in the car
wear colours that clash
dance as fast as I can
wear silly hats
        and my Grandmother's old fur coat
make snow angels
wear rubber boots
pick dandelions.

## A Prayer for Women

May change come.
May girls and women around the world
    grow up in secure and loving environments,
Free from violence, ridicule, and rape,
Free to make their own life choices,
Free to go to school,
Free to know the joys of a life fulfilled.

## Finding Strength to Change

May I relinquish my fear of change and remember —

> I always have options.
> I can develop a clear vision to see my options.
> I have the strength to alter my circumstances
>     and control my responses.
> I can surround myself with positive and
>     supportive people.
> I am embraced in the circle of the divine.

## Finding Strength to Face Illness

**For myself:**
In this frightening place of illness, may I find inner strength.

Blessed be my caregivers.
May I gather from them the light I need to carry on.
May I trust that my caregivers are making sound decisions about my care.
May I find a balance between the power to fight and the strength to let go.

**For others:**
In this frightening place of illness, may you find inner strength.

Blessed be your caregivers.
May you gather from them the light you need to carry on.
May you trust them and know that they are making sound decisions for you.
May you find a balance between the power to fight and the strength to let go.

## Finding the Strength to Face a Loved One's Illness

In this frightening place of illness, may I find the inner strength to care for you with compassion.
May I make wise decisions about your care.
May I truly listen to you.
May I find the power within me for both of us to carry on.
May our conversations be authentic.
May I be present when I am with you.
May I remember to listen instead of talk.
May I remember to touch.
May I find a balance between letting you fight and letting you go.

## Traveling To and From Work

Blessed be the minutes that I have to myself as I travel to and from work.
This time is a gift,
A time to practice being present in the moment,
A time to give thanks,
A quiet time before I face the expectations of my job and family.

## The To-Do List

May I find the strength
to rip up my to-do list
and let things slide.

Trusting that things will get done,
when they are meant to get done,
In good time,
whether I worry about them
or not.

## Sacred Spaces

We gather in the praise of sacred spaces,
the places where we feel a connection to the divine.
The quiet places where we feel a sense of reverence,
solitude, and inner peace.

May we cherish those spaces in our lives where the
layer between our world and the unseen world of
energies is paper-thin.

May we honour the need for sacred space in each
other, acknowledging that everyone has a different
relationship to the sacred, and that the places that
bring us close to the divine will be different for each of
us.

## Remembrances

I give thanks for the things that bring me closer to the
ones who are with me in spirit only;

My mother's handwritten recipes, covered in her
fingerprints, the cards transparent with shortening
and crusted with sugar.

My grandmother's wooden box of hankies, still
smelling of lavender, lovingly tatted around each
edge.

The sepia photograph of my seventeen-year-old
grandfather in his war uniform, as he prepared to
leave for Europe.

My father's black woolen overcoat that I wore for
years after he died, the sleeves too long and the lining
frayed.

I give thanks for the energy that lingers on the things
our loved ones have left behind.

## The Wisdom of Goose Bumps

I am grateful for the insight of goose bumps.

They rise on my bare skin at the touch of a gentle summer breeze.
They rise to the touch of my lover's hand on my neck.

The enthusiastic hug of a child,
the light dancing on the water,
the fluid colours of Monet's water lilies,
the movements of a modern dance,
the rise and fall of a Puccini aria,
bring goose bumps in waves of joy.

Goose bumps of reverence come
when energies align to announce
the presence of the divine.

May my goose bumps remind me to pay attention;
to be present,
and to honour my body's acknowledgment
of the divine.

## In Praise of Hands (1)

I give thanks for hands.

The newborn's hand that grasps the mother's finger, finding warmth and comfort outside the womb.

The hand of a small child finding reassurance from the strength and wisdom of a parent's hand.

The hand that offers the first gentle gesture of a relationship.

The hand of someone who is dying and longing for a reassuring touch.

## In Praise of Hands (2)

I am grateful for my hands,
Skillful and hard working.

Smoothing wrinkled sheets,
Cutting vegetables,
Rolling out pie dough,
Sorting cutlery,
Sewing on a button,
Ironing a shirt,
Hammering,
Cleaning up broken glass,
Typing,
Arranging flowers,
Diapering a baby.

All day long,
Serving me and serving others.

Blessings on my hands.

## Prayer for a Newborn Child

May blessings rest upon this infant.

May the innocence of this newborn child be shielded from ugliness and hopelessness.

May the life lessons this child learns be filled with warmth and tenderness.

May gentleness and kindness follow this child all of his/her days.

May the journey before this child be filled with enduring grace and love.

May this child be at peace in this world.

May this child experience good health.

May this child live in a state of gratitude.

May this child live in a sense of wonder.

## Teenagers

When I look into teenagers' eyes,
May I see their holy light,
For they are sacred beings struggling to find their
place in the world.

Even though they may turn away,
I must remember that they are still children in
growing bodies,
Needing me to create a safe and secure place for them
in the world.

May I see beyond their rejection of me and my ideas
And remember that they need me even though they
pretend they don't,
And are seeking my approval even though they seem
to not care.

May I be supportive without being judgmental.
May offer guidance without being critical.
May I let them make their own decisions, knowing
that there will be times when they fail.
May I forgive myself when I fail.

May I listen carefully to what they say and always
respond with kindness and respect,
For it is only when I model kindness and respect
That I will receive them in return.

## House of Cards

There is a calendar inside my head.
It lives there
with a host of appointments,
a whirlwind of details.
May I find stillness in my restless brain.

I am the responsible one.
I hold the schedules in my bathrobe
While I wear my slippers
and make sleepy-eyed coffee.
May I find stillness in my restless brain.

Each of my days are numbered squares,
carefully stacked children's blocks,
ready to topple over
with the weight of the little scrawls and etchings.
May I find stillness in my restless brain.

The tasks line up
like small soldiers in a row,
proudly forming a list.
These uniformed burdens wait to be cancelled
with a black line, a satisfied scratch,
that never make the list shorter.
Each eliminated enterprise
replaced at the end of the line
with another arrogant soldier.
May I find stillness in my restless brain.

I hold these fragile details, a house of cards.
May I find stillness in my restless brain.

## The Weight of the Moon

When my ovaries begin to tire,
When unpredictable rushes of hormonal angst
overpower me,
When my body becomes toxic and struggles beneath
the weight of the moon,
When the cycle of bliss becomes the cycle of suffering,
When I flash with heat, headaches cloud my brain,
and sleep eludes me,
May I be kind to myself and respond to my body's
needs.
May I honour this journey to my place of womanly
wisdom.

## Viruses

I am grateful for the insight that viruses grant me:

When to slow down and pay attention to my body's needs;

That I am vulnerable even to the smallest microbes and humbled by their power to bring me down.

When I try to outsmart them I soon realize that I cannot.

May I remember to be kind to myself.

## Swimming Laps

With gratitude I swim each stroke and bring forth the
joy that lives within me.
I give thanks for my body.
I am one with the water.

I give thanks for my inner and outer strength.
I am one with the water.

I give thanks for the blood coursing through my veins
that brings me power and energy.
I am one with the water.

I give thanks for the rhythm of the laps.
May it calm my chaotic mind.
I am one with the water.

I give thanks for the weightlessness of my body.
I am one with the water.

I give thanks for the gentle embrace of the soothing
liquid through which I glide.
May it soothe my aches and pains.
I am one with the water.

## Body Prayer

May blessings embrace my body.

May grace wash over my aches and pains.

I bless the parts of me that sag.

I bless the marks from my pregnancies that hug my stomach.

I bless my veins that have crept to the surface of my skin to make themselves known to me. May I greet them every morning in gratitude.

Each day, may I celebrate the work that my body has done for me and the things in life that my body has made possible.

Each day, may I honour the things that my body has taught me about my limitations.

May I listen to my body when it tells me to slow down, and may I celebrate the moments when it provides me with the energy to do the things that I need to do.

May I find the infinite beauty in my aging body and celebrate my body as a vessel in which sacred energies and divinity reside.

## Looking After a Sick Animal

Gentle friend, may you find strength in my tender words.

As I stroke your fur, may you know you mean the world to me.

I see the fear and pain in your eyes.

When I look at you, may you feel the love I have for you.

May I make wise decisions about your care.

## Divorce

May I no longer cling to my future plans and dreams that include *We*.

May I imagine a world for myself that finds peace in *I*.

May the relationship that I forge with my former spouse be constructive.

May it include a deep respect and understanding of the needs of our children.

May their needs come before our own.

## Banishing Negativity

May I surround myself with positive energy.

May I find room within me only for affirmations.

May I banish all negativity and oppressive thought
and call forth joy
to fill up the spaces left behind.

# Communal Prayers

## Prayer to the Wind

We hear the voice of the great spirit in the wind, and it comforts us.

We gather in praise of wind,
Of the air that flows around us.

Wind moves, and we harness it.
Yet we cannot control it.
It teaches us to be flexible.

We recognize its unpredictability and honour its sheer force.
It can fuel the fires of our planet and exert its destructive energy.

Yet it also reminds us of a divine presence
We feel that very presence in the small hot breath of our infants,
In the last shallow, sour inhalations of our dying loved ones,
And the sobbing gasps of our hurt children.

The spirit of the wind exerts its presence
Yet in its mystery we do not know where it comes from or where it goes.

Wind erodes mountains and teaches us that things must change,
Like the autumn breezes that scatter leaves and usher in the changing season.

It teaches us about permanence.
The wind has always been and will always be.

The wind has the strength to carry dust from the
distant Sahara to the smog-filled skies of our cities.

It carries pollen to continue life.
It carries the scent of our deceased loved ones.
It carries our words.

We give thanks for the wind.

## Compassion

As we turn to prayer, may we still our thoughts and calm our minds.

May we first extend compassion to ourselves. We all have regrets, we all have shortcomings, we all have painful memories, we all have suffered losses. May we open wide our arms of acceptance and forgiveness so that even for these few moments we may feel the blessing of self-compassion.

As we draw the circle wider, may we know compassion for our loved ones, those close by, those far away, those estranged from us, those gone from us, those we remember now by name...

May we have compassion for those in our social and work communities, those who disagree with us, those who need our care, those we sometimes wish would go away, those we remember now by name...

May we turn a compassionate mind to those who walk the streets of our towns and cities and the countryside, those who have little, those who have much, those who break the law, those who keep it. May we keep from judging or envying others.

It is sometimes easier to have compassion for those in need in the Horn of Africa, or Syria, or Attawapiskat than for those wrapped in sleeping bags lying on the downtown sidewalks. May we be mindful of the injustice suffered by millions of men, women and children.

May we have compassion for ourselves as we learn how to live and care and love in a world that keeps changing.

## In the Face of Adversity

We cannot always choose our situation,
        but we can challenge our perceptions.
May we acknowledge that even our fury is holy,
        and adversity has its own divine light.
May we honour the gentle peace that radiates from
        those who choose stillness.
May we  meditate on kindness
        as we work for change.

## Prayers of the People

*Holy mystery:*

We want to pray, we need to pray. Yet sometimes we cannot pray because we can't imagine to whom or to what we pray.

May we know that the urge to pray is prayer itself, that even when we can't find the right words, the struggle for words is prayer itself.

Let us be still, and breathe, knowing that the breath of life is divine, that we live in the divine and that the divine lives in us.

The urge to pray is sometimes rooted in gratitude. When a baby is born healthy and loved, when the bare November trees reveal their symmetry against a glowing violet sunset, when a loved one regains health, when we see November mists rising over the fields and streets, or when we crunch into a fresh Ida Red apple.

When we see a new grandchild for the first time, when we have coffee with our dearest friend, when our adult child returns safely from long travel, when a long awaited baby is conceived, our hearts burst with the overwhelming need to express our gratitude.

And so we remember—now, in silence—some of those moments of overwhelming gratitude.

\* \* \*

And sometime the urge to pray is rooted in fear and pain, when "Oh help!" is all we can say. When illness, despair, loss, injustice, and loneliness hold us in their grip, may we feel the sustaining presence of the divine within. May we gather strength one minute at a time as we breathe in courage and breathe out fear.

Sometimes the urge to pray comes from our concern for others. When families are cast into unknown territory by the loss of jobs, when depression and ill health break relationships, when children live in fear in their own homes, when adolescents seem lost to themselves and to their families, when our planet suffers by our own hands, we cry out in anger and frustration. Now, in this stillness, let us ask for comfort and courage for all who suffer, those whose names we know, and those whose names we don't know.

Sometimes the urge to pray comes from feelings of awe. The wonder of a starry night, the wonder that we are here at all on this earth, the wonder of birth and transformation, the wonder of the power of love and forgiveness. May we open ourselves to that awe and wonder which is prayer.

And now, like St. Francis, we pray.

*May we be instruments of peace;*
*where there is hatred, let us sow love;*
*where there is injury, pardon;*
*where there is doubt, faith;*
*where there is despair, hope;*
*where there is darkness, light;*
*and where there is sadness, joy.*
*May we not so much seek to be consoled as to console;*
*to be understood, as to understand;*
*to be loved, as to love;*
*for it is in giving that we receive,*
*it is in pardoning that we are pardoned.*

*For ever and ever,*
*Amen.*

# Prayer Stones

In the ancient tradition of reciting prayers while counting off beads, like the rosary or meditation beads, we offer the following prayers to say with simple stones.

Gather five stones. They can be stones that have special meaning, or simply stones you have found in your surroundings. Select one smooth stone, one rough stone, one flat, one round, and one of your choice. Put them in a bowl, bag, or your pocket.

Learn by heart the prayer for each stone.

## Rough

May I find wisdom in my darkness.

## Smooth

May I be still and know my inner strength.

## Round

May I feel divine light in and around me.

## Flat

I am grateful in this moment for _____.

## Chosen Stone

May I _____(Insert your own intention.)

*Melanie and Katharine*

# Authors & Acknowledgements

**Katharine Smithrim**, PhD, has kept alive her connection to the mainstream liberal church by reading contemporary and feminist theology and participating in the same women's spirituality group with co-author Melanie for 20 years. She is a singer, writer, walker, swimmer, sewer (garments, not pipes), and Professor *Emerita* of arts education at Queen's University, Kingston, Canada.


**Melanie Craig-Hansford** cannot bring herself to attend mainstream church anymore but is still an active member of a women's spirituality group after 20 years. Melanie is a Teacher-Librarian at a high school in Kingston, Ontario. Melanie received a B.F.A. and B.Ed. from the Nova Scotia College of Art and Design. She is a freelance writer and has contributed over one hundred editorial columns to *The Kingston Whig Standard*. Melanie likes to walk, swim, paint, and read.

Our thanks to Sandy and David.

And to our women's group:

Mary Carlson
Mary Davis
Terry Hudson
Margorie Levan
Helen Mathers
Marg Quigley
Joan Simeon

*Katharine Smithrim*
*Melanie Craig-Hansford*
*Kingston, Ontario*
*August, 2012*

Wintergreen Studios Press is an independent literary press. It is affiliated with the not-for-profit educational retreat centre, Wintergreen Studios, and supports the work of Wintergreen Studios by publishing works related to education, culture, and the environment.

www.wintergreenstudiospress.com
www.wintergreenstudios.com

15003754R00041

Made in the USA
Charleston, SC
12 October 2012